Superhero Superstars
Tom Holland

by Martha London

FOCUS READERS®

BEACON

www.focusreaders.com

Focus Readers is distributed by North Star Editions:
sales@northstareditions.com | 888-417-0195

Produced for Focus Readers by Red Line Editorial.

Photographs ©: Xavier Collin/Image Press Agency/Sipa USA/AP Images, cover, 1; DC/MediaPunch/MediaPunch/IPX/AP Images, 4; Shutterstock Images, 6, 8, 12, 14, 19, 20-21, 22, 29; Stefan Rousseau/PA Wire URN:8486461/Press Association/AP Images, 11; Eric Charbonneau/Invision/Sony Pictures/AP Images, 16; RW/MediaPunch/MediaPunch/IPX/AP Images, 25, 26

Library of Congress Cataloging-in-Publication Data
Names: London, Martha, author.
Title: Tom Holland / by Martha London.
Description: Lake Elmo, MN : Focus Readers, 2021. | Series: Superhero
   superstars | Includes index. | Audience: Grades 4-6
Identifiers: LCCN 2019060248 (print) | LCCN 2019060249 (ebook) | ISBN
   9781644933701 (hardcover) | ISBN 9781644934463 (paperback) | ISBN
   9781644935989 (pdf) | ISBN 9781644935224 (ebook)
Subjects: LCSH: Holland, Tom, 1996---Juvenile literature. | Motion pictures
   actors and actresses--Great Britain--Biography--Juvenile literature.
Classification: LCC PN2598.H58 L66 2021 (print) | LCC PN2598.H58 (ebook)
   | DDC 791.4302/8092 [B]--dc23
LC record available at https://lccn.loc.gov/2019060248
LC ebook record available at https://lccn.loc.gov/2019060249

Printed in the United States of America
Mankato, MN
082020

About the Author

Martha London writes books for young readers full-time. When she isn't writing, she can be found hiking in the woods.

Table of Contents

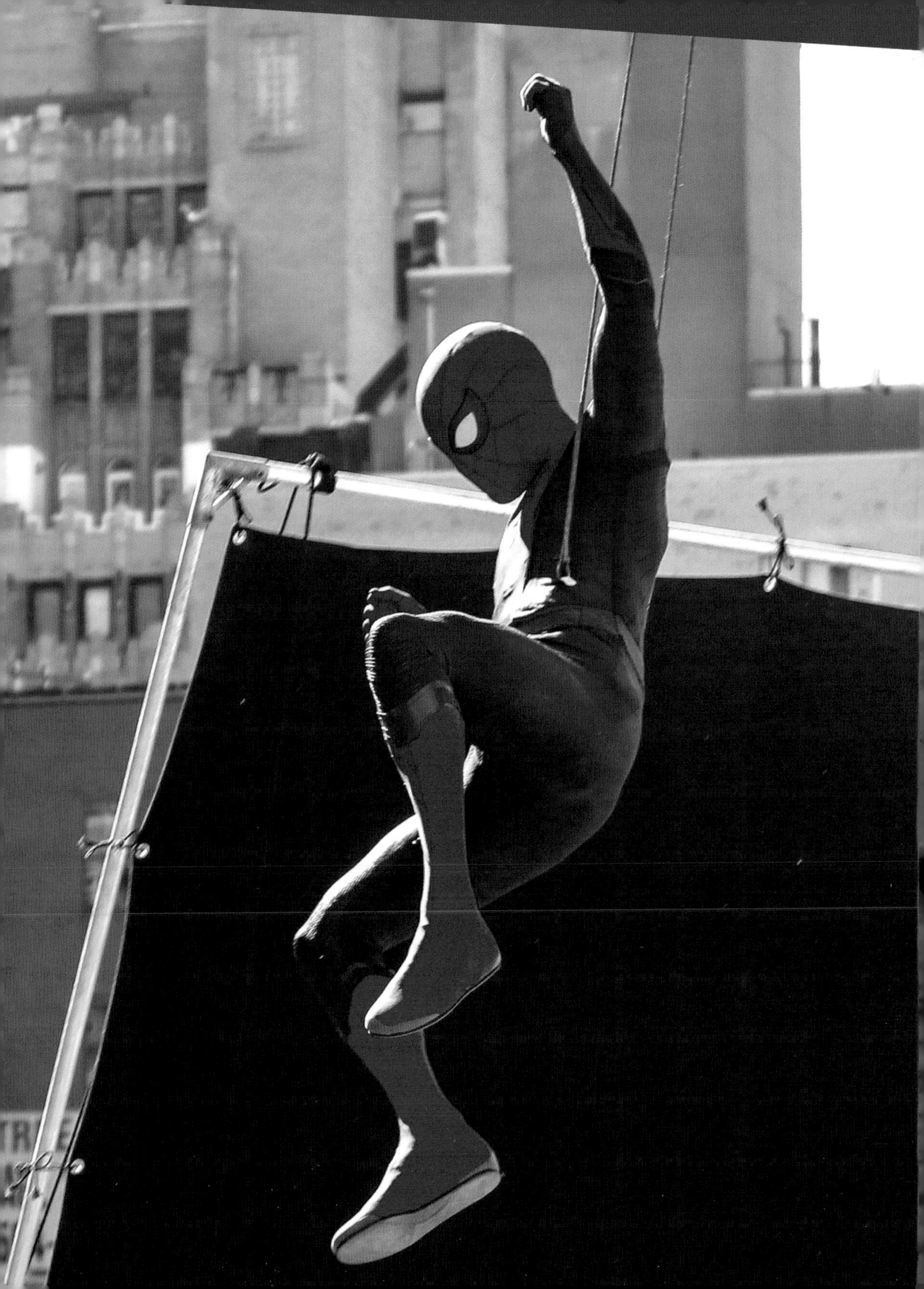

Chapter 1

Homecoming

Tom Holland sits near the end of a ledge. A Spider-Man mask covers his face. The **director** sits next to him. He explains the **scene** to Holland. Holland is going to fall off the ledge.

Holland did not do all of his own stunts. Here, a stunt double stands in for Holland during a tricky move.

 Spider-Man is popular around the world. The comics have been translated into many languages.

Holland holds on to a wire. The camera turns on. The wire pulls Holland off the ledge. Other wires steady him as he flips through the air.

Holland lands on a thick pad. A person is there to catch him. Holland gives the camera a thumbs-up. It was a good shot. The team gets ready to film the next one. Holland loves acting. He loves being Spider-Man.

Fun Fact

The first **live-action** Spider-Man TV show was filmed in 1977.

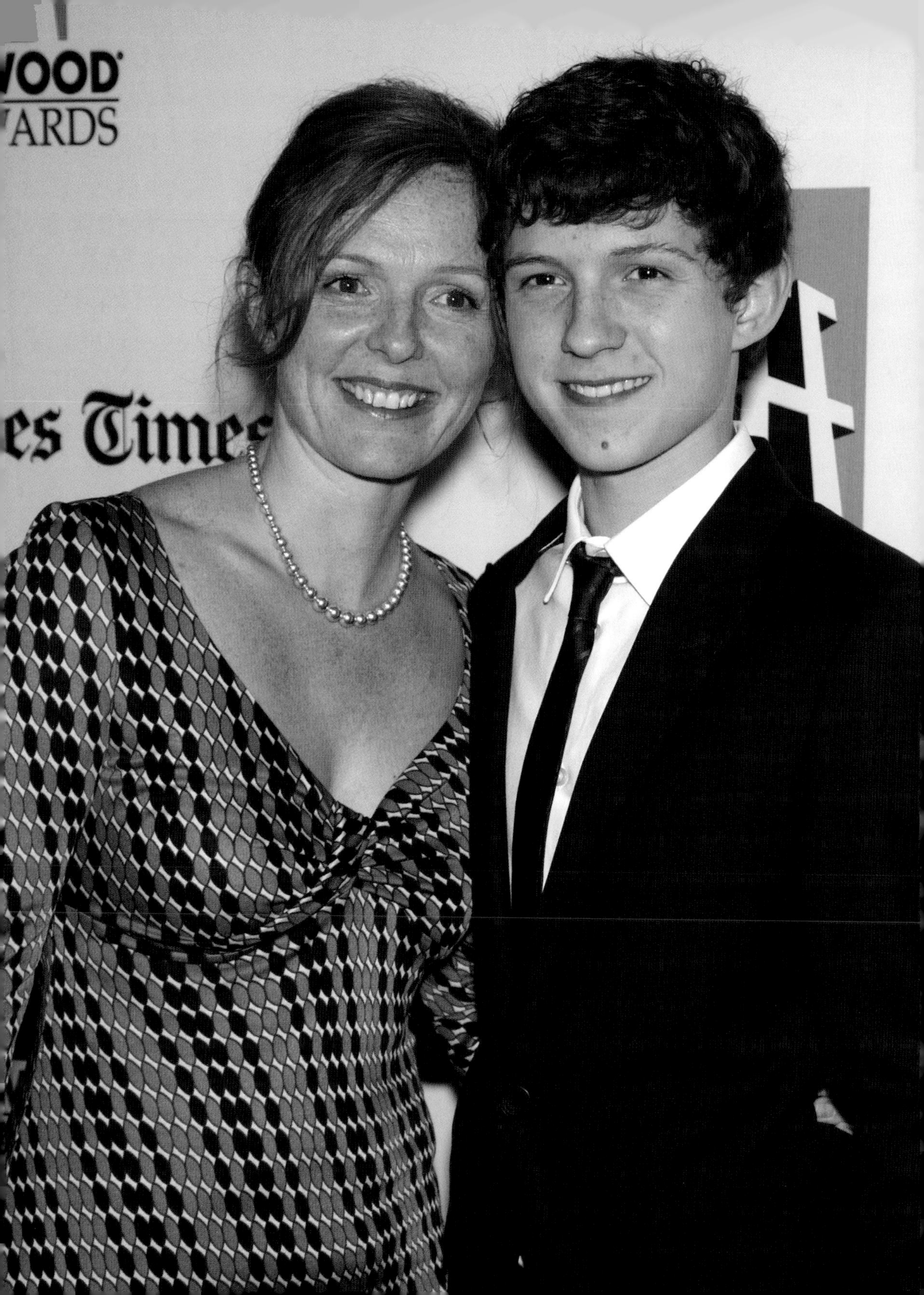

WOOD
ARDS
es Times

Chapter 2

Start Dancing

Tom Holland was born on June 1, 1996. He grew up in England. Tom's mom is a photographer. His dad is a comedian. His parents encouraged him to follow his dreams.

 Tom and his mom attend an awards show in 2012.

Tom loved dancing as a kid. He took hip-hop dance classes. When he was 10, his dance group entered a contest. A **choreographer** saw him dance. She worked with a theater company in London. The company was starting a new musical. It was about a male ballet dancer. The choreographer thought Tom would be a good fit.

Fun Fact

Tom has three younger siblings.

 Tom (far right) met the leader of the British government in 2010.

Tom still had to **audition**. He also needed to learn ballet. Tom worked hard. He took ballet classes for two years. After that, the musical director gave him a supporting **role**.

Holland jokes around with actor Will Smith. They worked together on the movie *Spies in Disguise*.

People loved Tom's performance in the musical. Less than three months after he joined the cast, Tom took over the lead.

Tom did not always know he wanted to be an actor. But he loved performing. He finished the musical in May 2010. He got his first movie role two months later. People who saw the movie liked his acting.

But Tom was still unsure if acting was what he wanted to do. Then, he started trying out for the role of Spider-Man. Tom knew he wanted to be a superhero.

Fun Fact

Tom learned he was the new Spider-Man from an Instagram post.

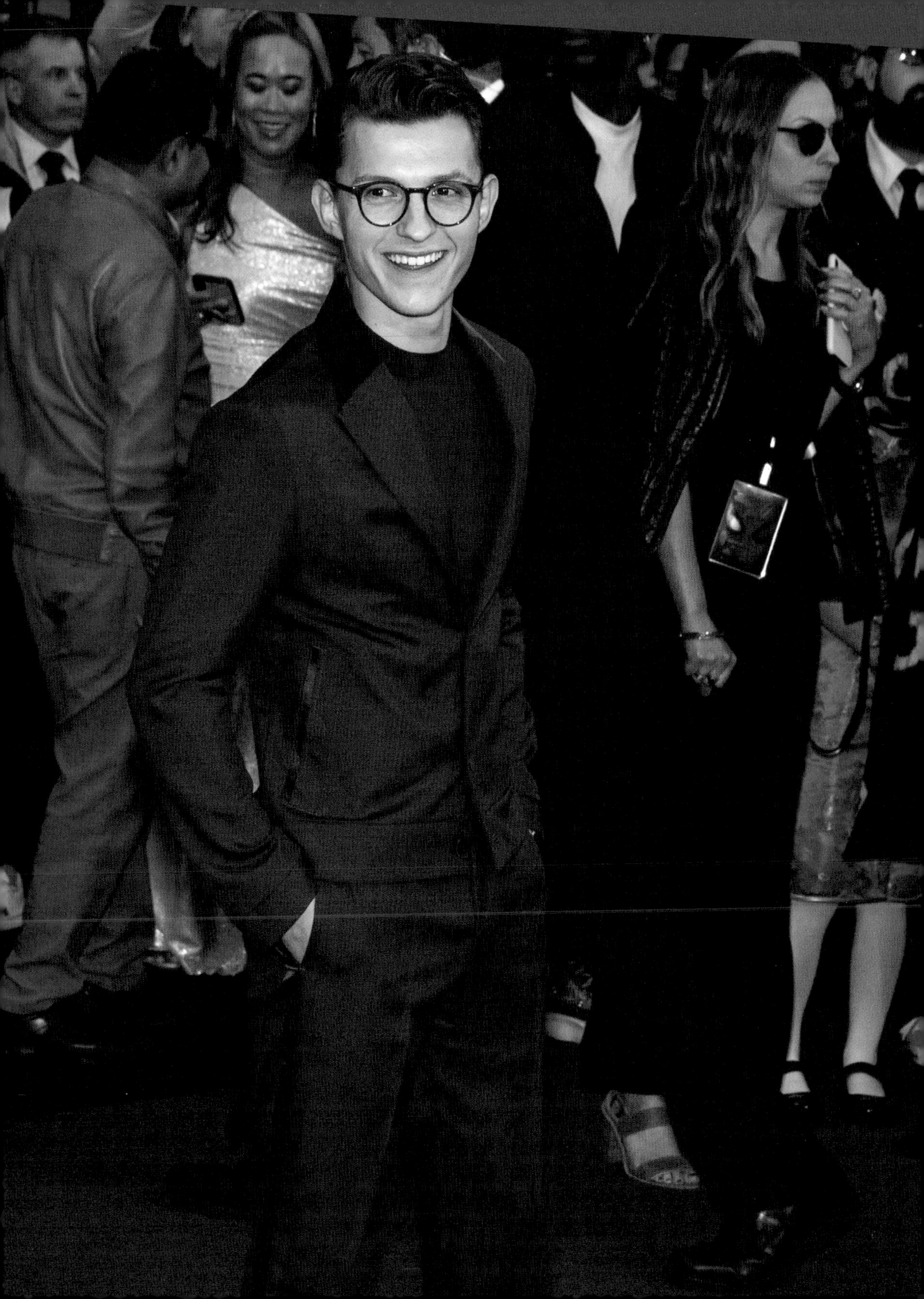

Chapter 3

Using His Fame for Good

Holland has become famous because of Spider-Man. But he doesn't take that fame for granted. He makes sure to give back to the community.

 Photographers take Holland's picture at the first showing of *Spider-Man: Far From Home*.

> **Holland and his family attend the first showing of *Spider-Man: Homecoming* in 2017.**

Holland's family created the Brothers Trust. This organization raises money to help charities around the world. Charities rely on **donations** to do their work. They use the money to help people in need. The Brothers Trust helps charities that don't get large donations. Some of the groups support childhood schooling. Other groups look for ways to treat certain illnesses.

Holland uses his fame to help raise money. One time, he offered a trip to the red carpet as a prize. The name of every person who donated to the Brothers Trust was put into a **raffle**. Holland picked one name.

That person and a friend joined Holland in Los Angeles. Many fans donated. They wanted a chance to meet Holland. The Brothers Trust raised a lot of money.

Holland helps people in other ways, too. For example, he joined the #IGiveASpit campaign. This

Fun Fact

One charity the Brothers Trust supports is the Lunchbowl Network. This charity feeds hundreds of kids who do not have families.

 Holland receives a thank-you card for the work the Brothers Trust did to help a community clinic.

movement helped people with

blood cancer. Because of his

fame, Holland can influence his

fans in good ways. He raises their

awareness of important causes.

Going Undercover

High school in the United States is different from school in England. Holland did not know what it was like to be an American student. But Spider-Man is a student in New York City.

The director had an idea. He sent Holland to a high school in New York City. Holland spent three days at the school. He learned what it was like to be a student in the United States. He talked to students. He asked them questions. None of the students knew who Holland was. He was able to act like a normal kid.

Holland and his two costars all play high school students.

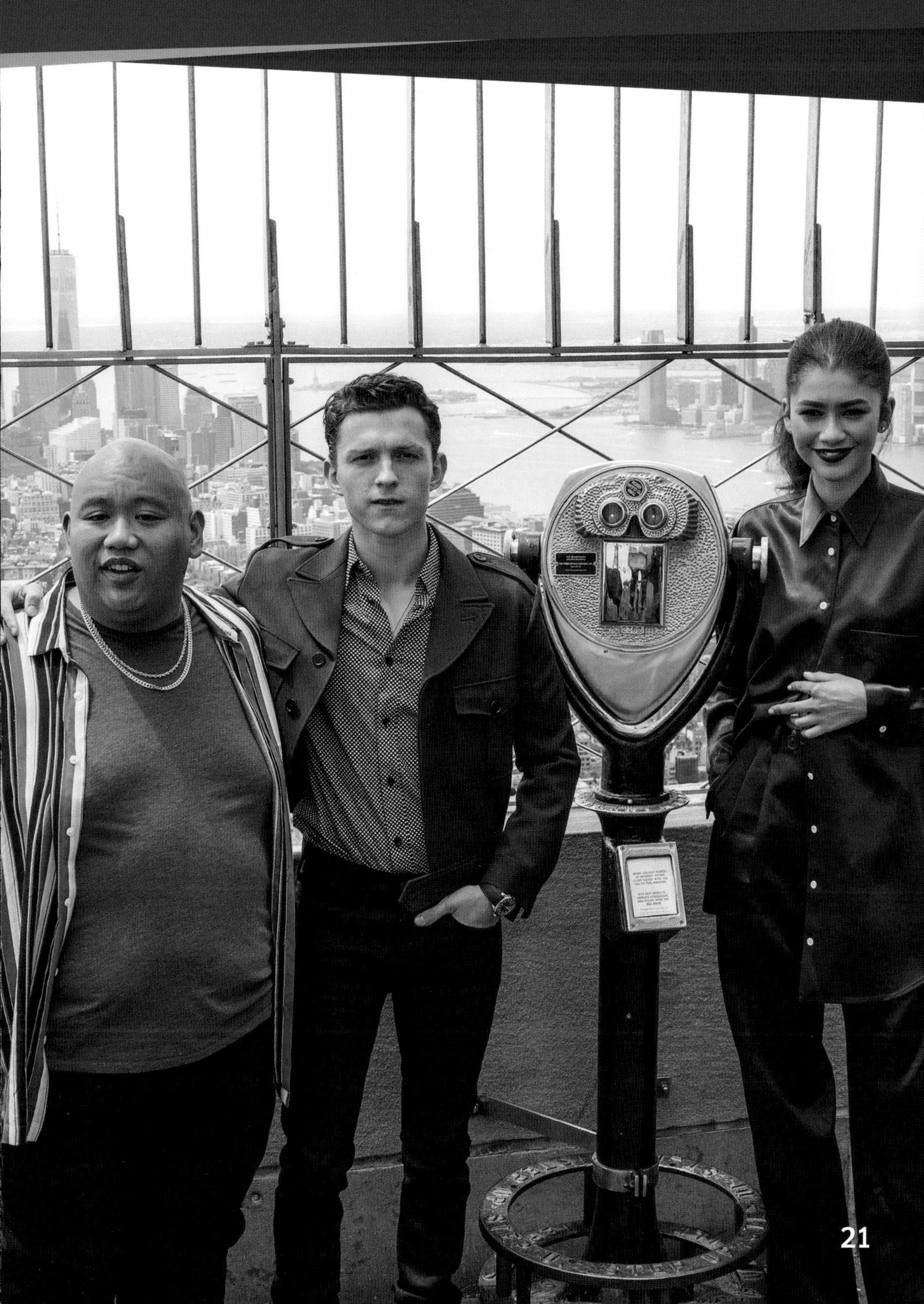

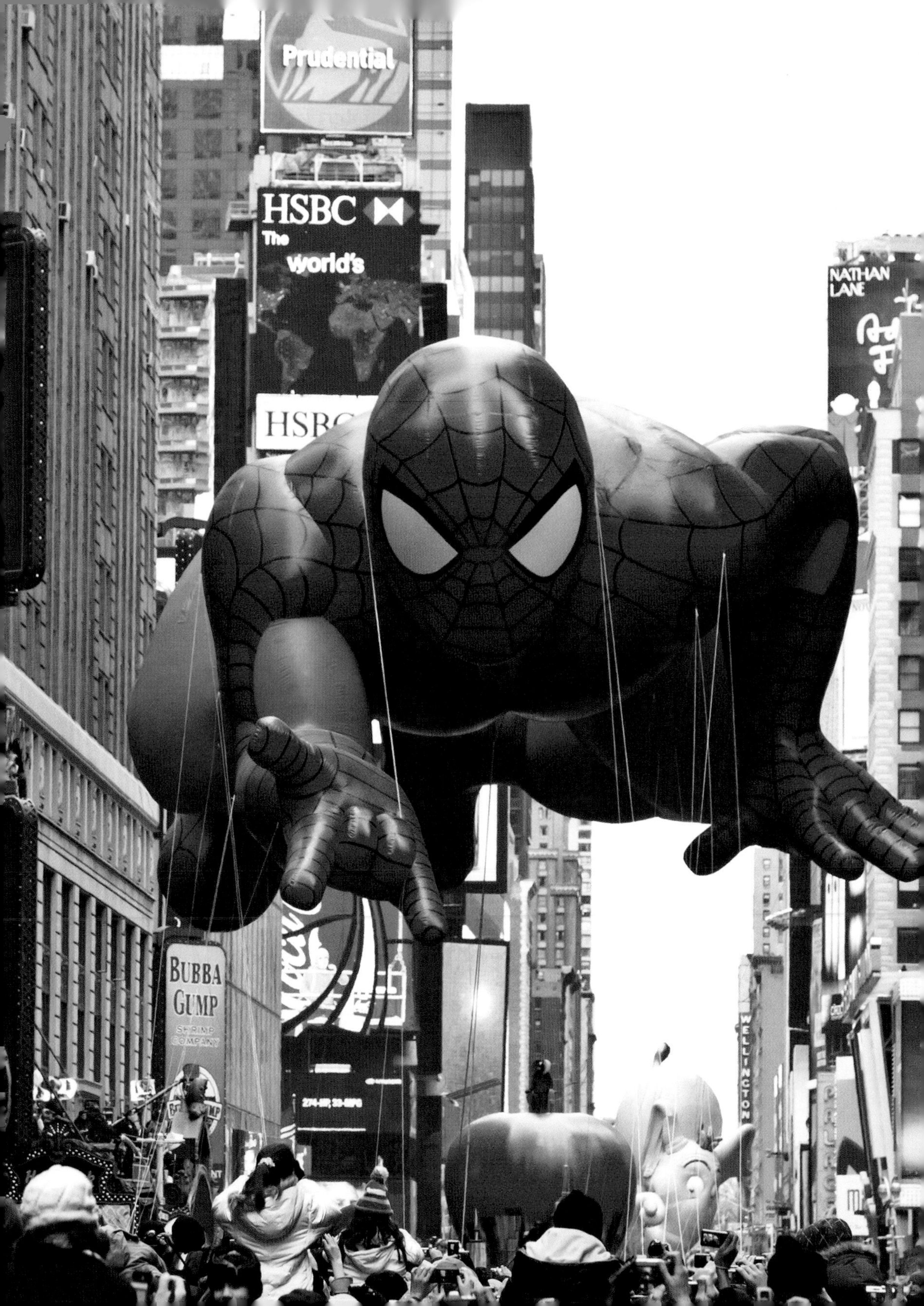
Prudential
HSBC
The world's
HSBC
NATHAN LANE
BUBBA GUMP
SHRIMP COMPANY
WELLINGTON

Chapter 4

Playing the Part

Holland is an important actor in the Marvel Cinematic Universe. He starred in Spider-Man movies in 2017 and 2019. He also appeared in *Captain America: Civil War* and two Avengers movies.

 Spider-Man is a well-known member of the Marvel Cinematic Universe.

Fans like that Holland is young. Past actors who played Spider-Man were older. Spider-Man is a high school student. Holland is close in age to the character.

Playing Spider-Man is not just about being young. The role takes strength and skill. In many scenes,

Fun Fact

Spider-Man gained his powers from a spider bite. But in real life, Holland is afraid of spiders.

 A stunt double pulls off a hard move with the help of wires.

Holland had to wear a harness. Wires attached to the harness. The wires lifted him into the air. In the movie, it looks like Holland is flying.

 Holland practices a move on set.

But harnesses can be hard to move in. Holland had to use his dance skills to help him do stunts.

Holland's dance training gave him strong stomach muscles. He used these muscles to stay balanced in the harness. Holland was able to move smoothly. He made it look easy. However, working with wires is hard.

Spider-Man was just the beginning for Holland. He has been in other movies. And he has many goals. He hopes to be a director someday. But for now, Holland is focusing on acting.

FOCUS ON
Tom Holland

Write your answers on a separate piece of paper.

1. Write a blog post talking about how Holland's dancing helped his acting.

2. Do you think actors should use their fame to help others? Why or why not?

3. When did Holland get his first movie role?
>   **A.** 1977
>   **B.** 2010
>   **C.** 2017

4. Why was it important for Holland to spend time in a US high school?
>   **A.** It helped him make friends in a new country.
>   **B.** It helped him finish his education.
>   **C.** It helped him act like a real US student.

5. What does **cast** mean in this book?

*Less than three months after he joined the **cast**, Tom took over the lead.*

    A. the furniture and backgrounds that make up the set of a play

    B. the dance movements in a performance

    C. the actors who perform in a play or movie

6. What does **influence** mean in this book?

*Because of his fame, Holland can **influence** his fans in good ways. He raises their awareness of important causes.*

    A. to control people with force

    B. to change how people think

    C. to act in a play or movie

Answer key on page 32.

Glossary

audition
To give a short performance as a test.

choreographer
A person who creates dance routines.

director
A person who is in charge of making a movie.

donations
Money given to a charity.

live-action
A movie or tv show that shows real people rather than animations or cartoons.

raffle
A way to raise money by selling tickets, picking one ticket randomly, and giving a prize to the person holding the ticket.

role
The part an actor plays in a television show or movie.

scene
A specific place and time during a movie or play.

To Learn More

BOOKS

Bray, Adam. *Marvel Studios Character Encyclopedia*. New York: DK Publishing, 2019.

Green, Sara. *Visual Effects*. Minneapolis: Bellwether Media, 2020.

Orr, Nicole K. *Tom Holland*. Kennett Square, PA: Purple Toad Publishing, 2017.

NOTE TO EDUCATORS

Visit **www.focusreaders.com** to find lesson plans, activities, links, and other resources related to this title.

Index

Answer Key: 1. Answers will vary; **2.** Answers will vary; **3.** B; **4.** C; **5.** C; **6.** B